Navigating Stagnation:
an ultimate guide to achieve your goals and master self-growth!

This isn't just another journal; it's a powerful tool designed to transform your mindset, ignite your focus, and build actionable strategies.

Whether you're looking to:

- Cultivate mindfulness
- Improve productivity
- Become more intentional
- Break through personal barriers

This journal is the perfect companion on your journey to self-improvement and healing.

-Dr. Christina Baker

Meraki Journey Family

This journal is meant to be paired with our book, 'Feeling Stuck in Life: *Breaking Free From Stagnation*'.

FSiL is the foundational guide that equips you with the tools and knowledge to truly break free from what's holding you back. It also provides deeper insights, unconventional methods, and practical lessons needed to identify and address the root causes of your stagnation.

In addition to the book, this *Strategic Journaling* helps with tracking your progress and reflecting on your journey.

Remember, each journal entry brings you one step closer to a more purposeful life.

Happy Journaling,

Meraki Journey Therapy Team

This journal includes 32 activities organized into 9 themes, all of which are aligned with the principles outlined in the book **FSiL.**

1. **Healing and Transformation** (Activities 1-7):
Begin your healing journey and embrace the process of transformation.

2. **Self-Awareness and Reflection** (Activities 8-14):
Explore your inner self and gain clarity on your thoughts and emotions.

3. **Boundaries and Alignment** (Activities 15-20):
Learn how to set healthy boundaries and align with your true self.

4. **Goal Setting and Planning** (Activities 21-23):
Create clear, actionable goals to move you forward.

5. **Support and Community** (Activities 24-25):
Reflect on the power of support and connection in your life.

6. **Creative Expression and Visualization** (Activities 26-27):
Tap into your creativity to envision the life you want.

7. **Gratitude and Mindfulness** (Activities 28-29):
Cultivate gratitude and stay present in your journey.

8. **Overcoming Mental Barriers** (Activity 30):
Break through the mental blocks that hold you back.

9. **Personal Growth and Empowerment** (Activities 31-32):
Step into your personal power and embrace your growth.

Healing and Transformation
Confronting your past and reshaping your narrative

Purpose: This theme focuses on facilitating personal healing and self-transformation.

Benefits: 1. Gaining insights into past traumas, and its effects on your life. **2.** Fostering resilience and empowerment to promote self-discovery and emotional release.

ACTIVITIES

1. **The Phoenix Reflection**
2. **Identifying Triggers and Trauma Responses**
3. **Embracing the Journey of Healing**
4. **Rewriting Trauma Narratives**
5. **The Breakthrough Plan (Phoenix Method)**
6. **Letting Go: Releasing What No Longer Serves You**
7. **The Link Between Trauma and Stagnation: Reconstruct Your Path**

1. The Phoenix Reflection

Prompt: What past experiences or behaviors have left you feeling stuck or stagnant?

Exercise:

Write down three major life events that has caused you to feel stagnant.

Be sure to include how each event has shaped you, and what lessons you can extract from those experiences.

2. Identifying Triggers & Trauma Responses

Prompt: What are some emotional or physical reactions you noticed when triggered by past traumas? How to control your emotions to minimize mental breakdowns?

Exercise: Create a list of common triggers. Pair each trigger with your corresponding emotional or physical responses to your experience.

Reflect on how recognizing your triggers and trauma responses can empower you to become more self-aware and intentional with your actions.

3. Embracing the Journey of Healing
Envisioning into Existence

Prompt: What does healing look like to you, and what does it require from you?

Exercise: Write a letter to yourself describing what your life will look and feel like after you've healed from your past traumas, letdowns, or disappointments.

In details, describe your emotional, mental, and physical state in this envisioned future.

4. Rewriting Trauma Narratives

Prompt: How has your trauma shaped your current life's story? What would your life look like if you rewrote the narrative?

Exercise:

Step 1: Write a brief summary of your life story through the lens of your trauma.

Step 2: Rewrite that summary through the lens of the strengths, lessons, and growth you've gained from those experiences.

What differences do you notice between the two summaries?

5. The Breakthrough Plan

Prompt: What area(s) of your life do you want to break free from? What is one step you can take <u>today</u> to move toward that goal?

Exercise:

Step 1: Write down a stagnant area (career, relationships, self-worth, etc.).

Step 2: Brainstorm at least three actionable steps to move forward.

Commit to one step at a time and track your progress weekly.

6. Letting Go: Releasing What No Longer Serves You

Prompt: What beliefs, behaviors, or relationships are holding you back from becoming the person you want to be? What emotional weight are you carrying that no longer serves you?

Exercise:

1. **Identifying Emotional Baggage:** Write down three things—whether habits, relationships, beliefs, or memories—that you feel are holding you back. Next to each one, describe how it impacts your daily life or personal growth.

2. **The Release:** After reflecting, write a letter to yourself stating specific beliefs or behavior that you're letting go of. In this letter:
   - Express gratitude for any lessons learned
   - Acknowledge the pain it caused
   - Release it from your life.

3. **Reflection Questions:**
   - How does it feel to let go of these things?
   - What space has this release create for new growth or healing in your life?

7. The Link Between Trauma and Stagnation

Prompt: In what ways have unresolved trauma and self-sabotage kept you from moving forward? How has trauma influenced the choices you make and the actions you take in your life?

Exercise:

1. **Identifying Unresolved Trauma:** Reflect on a moment or experience from your past that still feels unresolved. Write down the event and describe any emotions, thoughts, or patterns that continue to arise from it. How has this trauma shaped your behavior or your ability to pursue your goals?

2. **Recognizing Self-Sabotage:** Now, think about ways in which you may be sabotaging your own healing and progress. Are there habits or mindsets that keep you stuck (ex: procrastination, fear of failure, negative self-talk)? Write down three self-sabotaging behaviors that you've noticed within yourself.

3. **Reflection Questions:**
   - What is the root cause of your self-sabotaging actions?
   - How do these behaviors protect or serve you? (*Self-sabotage is often a defense mechanism.*)
   - How are these behaviors connected to your unresolved trauma?

4. **Reconstructing Your Path:** After identifying the trauma and how it has led to self-sabotage, write a new plan for moving forward. For each self-sabotaging behavior, come up with <u>one</u> positive action that you can take to replace it.

Focus on actions that will promote healing and growth (ex: setting smaller, achievable goals, being kinder to yourself, or seeking support).

5. **Action Step:** Commit to working on one specific behavior this week. Track how it feels to replace the self-sabotaging habit with the new positive action, and journal any emotional shifts or progress.

2. Self-Awareness and Reflection

Purpose: This theme encourages you to cultivate self-awareness and regularly reflect on your thoughts, emotions, and behaviors.

Benefits: 1. Engaging in reflective exercises will help you to understand your emotional landscape better. **2.** Lead to improved emotional regulation and clarity in navigating life's challenges.

8. Checking in with Yourself (Weekly Reflection)
9. Daily Gratitude for Resilience
10. The Trauma Timeline: Mapping Your Journey
11. The Inner Child Dialogue
12. Strategic Journaling Exercise: Channeling Your Inner Versions
13. Protecting Your Mental Stability
14. Mind-Body Connection: Somatic Healing

8. Checking in with Yourself (Weekly Reflection):

Prompt: In what ways have you honor your healing process this week? Is there anything else that you can do to offer yourself more <u>patience</u> or <u>self-compassion</u>?

Exercise: Use this prompt at the end of each week to reflect on your journey.

<u>Consider:</u>

1. What's working well for you and your healing process.

2. Where adjustments are needed to continue progressing in your healing.

9. Daily Gratitude for Resilience:

Prompt: What <u>strengths</u> have you developed as a result of surviving difficult times?

Exercise: Write down three things you're grateful for each day.

Your key focus with this exercise is things that have influenced your <u>resilience</u>, <u>strength</u>, and <u>ability to grow</u> through challenges.

10. The Trauma Timeline: Mapping Your Journey.

Connecting your past experiences to their current feelings of stagnation.

Prompt: What key events have shaped your experiences with trauma and stagnation? How have these events influenced your path?

Exercise:

1. **Create a Timeline:** Draw a horizontal line on a page to represent your life journey. Mark significant events related to your trauma and periods of stagnation, placing them chronologically along the timeline.

2. **Reflect on Each Event:** For each event, write a brief description of how it impacted you at that time. *Consider how it has influenced your current beliefs, behaviors, and feelings about yourself.*

3. **Identify Patterns:** Look for patterns or recurring themes in your timeline. Are there certain triggers or situations that frequently lead to feelings of stagnation or self-sabotage?

4. **Reframe the Narrative:** Next to each event, write down a <u>lesson learned</u>, or a <u>strength gained</u>. Have you grown or adapted as a result of these experiences?

11. The Inner Child Dialogue

Prompt: What does your inner child need to hear from you? How can you nurture or support this part of yourself to accelerate healing?

Exercise:

1. **Visualize Your Inner Child:** Take a moment to close your eyes and imagine yourself as a child. What do you see? What emotions arise when you think about specific childhood experiences?

2. **Write a Letter:** Begin a dialogue with your inner child by writing a letter. Start with: "Dear [Childhood name]".

   - Express love, understanding, and validation.
   - Acknowledge your inner child's feelings, fears, and experiences without judgment.

3. **Ask Questions:** After your initial letter, switch perspectives. Write a response from your inner child's point of view.

   - What does younger you want to express to you?
   - What does younger you need from you now as an adult?
   - How can you provide those things to your younger self?

4. **Reflection Questions:**

   - What insights did you gain from this dialogue?

12. (Part 1) Channeling Your Inner Versions

Prompt: How can you transform your thoughts and emotions through strategic journaling? What insights can you gain by engaging with different versions of yourself?

Instructions:

1. **Acknowledge Your Inner Versions:** Begin by recognizing that multiple versions of you exist within. These can include feelings of happiness, sadness, anger, bravery, intelligence, etc.

2. **Identify Your Current Version:** Which version of you needs to express themselves right now? Is it anger, anxiety, happiness, or something else? *Write down your answer.*

3. **Uninterrupted Expression:** Stay true to that identified version. Write freely for 10-15 minutes without interruption, allowing this version of you to express thoughts and feelings. Let your pen flow, capturing everything without judgment.

4. **Determine the Ideal Respondent:** Think about the type of person best suited to address what you have written. Is it an intelligent, optimistic, or wise version of yourself? *Write down who this version is.*

5. **Channel the Respondent:** Now, channel this version of yourself. What would this version of you say or do after reading a journal entry like your current one? *Without judgement: Pay attention to the words and emotions conveyed.*

6. **Respond:** Before responding, set a reminder to revisit this journal entry in a day, week, or month. Then, write a letter to yourself, in response to your first letter.

12. (Part 2) Channeling Your Inner Versions

Self-Reflection

- Has your perspective shifted since you wrote the initial entry?

- What new wisdom or advice did you now offer yourself?

- Did giving yourself sometime before responding influenced they way you responded?

- Has this process has change your view of the situation?

- How can you integrate these insights into your life moving forward?

- What steps can you take to nurture the version of yourself that needs support?

- What did you learn about your <u>emotional landscape</u> through this exercise?

- How can engaging with different versions of yourself help you in navigating challenges or stagnation in the future?

13. Protecting Your Mental Stability

Prompt: What does mental stability mean to you, and what steps do you currently take to protect it?

Key Focus: Recognizing stressors, setting boundaries, and creating a plan to nurture mental well-being.

Exercise:

1. **Identify Stressors:** Write down three things or relationships that have caused you to feel mentally unstable or emotionally drained in the past month.

2. **Boundaries for Stability:** For each stressor, list one boundary you can establish to protect your mental stability. *This could be setting limits on time, energy, or emotional investment in a particular area.*

3. **Stability Plan:** Create a "**Mental Stability Protection Plan**". Write down three practices or habits that help you maintain your mental stability (ex: mindfulness, taking time for self-care, disconnecting from negative influences).

14. Mind-Body Connection: Somatic Healing
Trauma often resides in the body as well as the mind

Key Focus: Calming the nervous system and reducing physical manifestations of trauma.

Prompt: How does your body feel when you're anxious or triggered? How can you use this awareness to care for yourself?

Exercise: Practice somatic techniques mentioned in **Feeling Stuck in Life**. Then, journal how your body and mind feels before and after practicing the techniques.

3. Boundaries and Alignment

Purpose: **1.** This theme emphasizes the importance of establishing healthy boundaries. **2.** Ensuring alignment in relationships and personal goals.

Benefits: **1.** Learning to recognize, and set necessary boundaries while evaluating your relationships.
2. Promoting healthier connections and a supportive environment that aligns with your values.

15. Setting Healthy Boundaries
16. The Power of 'No'
17. The Boundary Blueprint
18. Intentional Alignment: Recognizing Misalignment
19. The Alignment Assessment

15. Setting Healthy Boundaries

Prompt: In what areas of your life do you feel that your boundaries are weak or non-existent?

Exercise: List areas where boundaries need strengthening (ex: work, relationships, personal time).

For each, write one specific action you can take to set a healthier boundary.

16. The Power of 'No':

Prompt: In what situations do you struggle to say 'no'? How can saying 'no' serve your well-being?

Exercise: List five scenarios where saying "no" would honor your boundaries.

Reflect on how you can practice this moving forward.

17. The Boundary Blueprint

Prompt: What boundaries do you need to set to protect your mental and emotional well-being? How can you communicate these boundaries effectively?

Exercise:

1. **Identify Boundaries:** Write down areas in your life where you feel your boundaries are being crossed. *This could be in relationships, work, or personal time.*

2. **Define Your Needs:** For each area, articulate what you need in order to feel <u>safe</u> and <u>respected</u>. *Be clear about what behaviors you will not tolerate and what you need from others.*

3. **Create a Communication Plan:** Draft a script for how you will communicate these boundaries to the relevant people. *Refer back to* **Feeling Stuck in Life** *for deeper guidance.*

4. Reflection Questions:
- What fears do you have about setting these boundaries?
- How can you address them?
- What steps will you take to reinforce these boundaries once they are set?

18. Intentional Alignment: Recognizing Misalignment

Prompt: Reflect on a current relationship or connection in your life where you feel misaligned. What areas of this connection feel out of sync with your goals, values, or behaviors?

Exercise:

1. **The Alignment Check:** Visualize the relationship.

   - On one side of the paper, write down your goals, values, and actions.
   - On the other side, write down the goals, values, and actions of the person or environment involved.
   - Compare both sides.

   Read **Feeling Stuck in Life** for a deeper understanding

2. **Reflection Questions:**

   - Where are each sides misaligned from the other?
   - How has this misalignment affected your emotional well-being or sense of progress in life?

3. **Action Step:** Write down two practical changes you could make to bring this connection into better alignment (ex: setting boundaries, having a conversation about shared values, or re-evaluating the relationship).

19. The Alignment Assessment

Prompt: How aligned are you with your values, goals, and the people in your life? What areas need adjustment?

Exercise:

1. **Create an Alignment Matrix:** Draw a grid with three columns: **Values, Goals,** and **Relationships.** List your core values in the first column, your current goals in the second, and significant relationships in the third.

2. **Assess Alignment:** For each entry, rate on a scale of 1-10 how aligned you feel it is with your life.

Rate:

- 1-3: Misaligned
- 4-6: Somewhat aligned
- 7-10: Aligned

3. **Reflection Questions:**

- Which areas scored the lowest?
- What changes can you make to improve alignment?
- Are there values that you're not living in accordance with? How can you bring those values into your daily life?

20. (Part 1) Setting and Maintaining Healthy Boundaries

When we're feeling stuck or stagnant, it can often be linked to a lack of healthy boundaries—whether with others or ourselves. This exercise will guide you through reflecting on your current boundaries, identifying where they might need strengthening, and creating a plan to uphold them.

Step 1: Reflect on Your Current Boundaries: (personal, professional, emotional, and physical):

- Are your current boundaries clear?
- Do you struggle to enforce them?

Write about any areas where your boundaries feel blurred or neglected.

Step 2: Identify Boundary Violations: Think about any recent moments when your boundaries were crossed or violated.

- How did it make you feel, and what was your response?
- Were you able to communicate your needs effectively, or did you struggle to assert yourself?

Step 3: Pinpoint Areas for Improvement: Reflect on the areas where you want to strengthen or adjust your boundaries. *Consider what you need to feel more __secure__, __balanced__, and __respected__ in your interactions with others and yourself.*

20. (Part 2) Setting and Maintaining Healthy Boundaries

Step 4: Create an Action Plan: Create a plan for how you will set and maintain healthy boundaries moving forward. *Be specific about the steps you'll take, and how you will communicate your boundaries to others.*

Step 5: Anticipate Challenges and Prepare Solutions: Identify potential obstacles you might face when enforcing your boundaries, and brainstorm solutions to overcome them.

Step 6: Reflection: Write about any insights or realizations that surfaced during this activity.

- How will you maintain your set boundaries moving forward?

4. Goal Setting and Planning

Purpose: This theme focuses on creating actionable plans for healing and personal growth; encouraging you to set clear, achievable goals and strategies to reach those goals.

Benefits: By developing structured approaches to your aspirations, you will feel empowered to take consistent actions toward your healing journeys and experience a sense of accomplishment.

21. Setting S.M.A.R.T. Goals for Healing and Growth
22. Coping Mechanism Plan: Building Your Toolkit
23. The Future Self Visualization

21. Setting S.M.A.R.T. Goals for Healing and Growth

Prompt: Reflect on a personal goal related to your healing or overcoming stagnation. Is this goal clear and actionable or does it feel vague and hard to achieve?

Exercise:

1. **Identify a Healing Goal:** Write down one goal that directly relates to your journey of healing from trauma or breaking free from stagnation. *This could be emotional, mental, or related to a personal boundary or habit you want to change.*

Example: "I want to reduce my anxiety around social interactions caused by past trauma."

2. **Break It Down Using S.M.A.R.T. Goals:**

Specific: What exactly do you want to achieve? *Be as detailed as possible.*

Measurable: How will you measure progress? What signs will show you're moving forward?

Achievable: Is this goal realistic? How can you break it down into manageable steps?

Relevant: Why is this goal important to your healing and growth?

Time-bound: Set a specific timeframe. When do you want to achieve this goal?

22. (Part 1) Coping Mechanism Plan: Building Your Toolkit

Prompt: What strategies can you implement to effectively cope with challenges and emotional distress in your life? How can you create a personalized coping mechanism plan?

Instructions:

1. **Identify Your Challenges:** Begin by listing specific challenges or stressors you're currently facing. *These can include feelings of anxiety, sadness, overwhelming responsibilities, or stagnation in certain areas of your life.*

2. **Recognize Your Emotions:** For each challenge listed, note the emotions associated with it.

- How does this challenge make you feel **physically** and **emotionally**?

Take a moment to reflect on the impact it has on your well-being.

3. Explore Existing Coping Strategies:

- What has helped you in the past?
- What strategies have you tried that didn't work?
- Why do you think they fell short?

22. (Part 2) Coping Mechanism Plan: Building Your Toolkit

4. New Coping Mechanisms:
New coping strategies that could be beneficial. Such as:
- Mindfulness practices
- Physical activities
- Creative outlets
- Journaling techniques
- Social interactions

Write down at least three new strategies you're interested in trying.

5. Create Your Coping Mechanism Plan:

Organize a personalized coping mechanism plan by listing a few strategies: whether from your existing and/or new lists.

Categories them based on when you might need them: **Immediate**, **Short-term**, or **Long-term**.

- **Immediate Coping:** Strategies you can use in the moment to alleviate stress (ex: deep breathing, quick walks).

- **Short-term Coping:** Strategies for managing stress over a few days (ex: journaling, talking to a friend).

- **Long-term Coping:** Ongoing practices to promote overall well-being (ex: regular therapy, exercise routine).

23. Visualize Your Future Self

Prompt: What does your life look like once you have healed from trauma and stagnation? Visualize your future self.

Exercise:

1. **Visualize Your Future Self:** Picture yourself five years from now, having overcome trauma and stagnation.
   - What are you doing?
   - How do you feel? Who is in your life?
   - What achievements have you made?

2. **Write a Letter <u>from</u> Your Future Self:** Write a letter addressed to your present self from this future perspective. *Include advice, encouragement, and the steps you took to get there.*

3. **Reflection Questions:**
   - What feelings arise when you envision this future?
   - How can you start taking steps toward this vision today?

4. **Action Step:** Choose one action that aligns with your future self and commit to doing it within the next week.

5. Support and Community

Purpose: This theme highlights the importance of seeking support from others and building a robust community, showcasing the role of relationships and resources in the healing process.

Benefits: Through these exercises, you will learn how to articulate your needs and reach out for help, fostering a sense of connection and reinforcing that you are not alone in your journey.

23. Seeking Support: Mapping Your Support System
24. Discovering Your Inner Voice: Trusting Your Own Guidance

23. (Part1) Seeking Support: Mapping Your Support System

Prompt: What areas of your life feel stagnant or challenging right now? How can you effectively seek support to help navigate these difficulties?

Instructions:

1. Identify Areas of Stagnation:

Begin by writing down the aspects of your life where you feel stuck or challenged. *This could include personal relationships, career, emotional health, or any specific goals.*

2. Acknowledge Your Feelings:

For each area of stagnation, jot down the feelings you experience. Are you feeling frustrated, overwhelmed, lonely, or confused? *Be honest and detailed in your descriptions.*

3. Determine Your Support Needs:

- Reflect on what type of support you need for each area identified. *Refer to* **Feeling Stuck in Life** *to learn about the 4 options.*
- Write down the specific support type you think is best suited for each area of stagnation.

23. (Part 2) Seeking Support: Mapping Your Support Systems

4. Communicate Your Needs:

List specific individuals or groups you can reach out to and note how you might communicate your needs to them.

- What will you say to express what you're going through?
- How can you ask for the support you need clearly and honestly?
- Write down any additional steps you need to take to facilitate this process (ex: scheduling a meeting, sending a message).

5. Reflection:

After reaching out for support, take time to reflect on the experience:

- How did it feel to express your needs?
- What was the response, and how did it impact your feelings of stagnation?

24. Discovering Your Inner Voice

Build a stronger connection to their inner wisdom

Prompt: When faced with difficult decisions, do you trust yourself to make the right choices, or do you find yourself relying on external validation?

Exercise:

1. **Connect with Your Inner Voice:** Ask yourself, "What does my inner voice need me to hear right now?" ***Without overthinking***, write down the first thoughts or feelings that come to you.

2. **Reflection Questions:**
   - How often do you listen to your inner voice or intuition?
   - Are there areas in your life where you doubt your own wisdom? Why?

3. **Trusting Your Wisdom:** Write down three situations where you've trusted your intuition and it led you to a positive outcome. Reflect on how trusting yourself in the future could empower you to make more aligned decisions.

4. **Action Step:** For the next week, practice pausing before making decisions—big or small. Take a few moments to listen to your inner guidance.

6. Creative Expression and Visualization

Purpose: This theme encourages the use of creative expression and visualization as tools for healing and self-discovery, unlocking deeper insights and fostering empowerment.

Benefits: Engaging in creative practices helps us to articulate our dreams and aspirations, enhancing motivation and providing a positive outlook on our healing process.

25. The Vision Board for Healing
26. Visualizing Your Phoenix Moment

25. The Vision Board for Healing

Prompt: What does your ideal healing journey look like? How do you envision your life once you break free from trauma and stagnation?

Exercise:

1. **Gather Materials:** Collect magazines, newspapers, or print images and words that resonate with your vision for healing. You can also use a digital platform if you prefer a digital vision board.

2. **Create Your Vision Board:** Cut out images, quotes, and words that represent your aspirations, strengths, and what healing means to you. Arrange them on a board or digital canvas in a way that feels cohesive and inspiring.

3. **Reflection:** As you create your vision board, reflect on the following questions:
   - What feelings do these images and words evoke?
   - How do they represent the person you aspire to be or the life you want to create?

4. **Action Plan:** Choose three specific actions you can take to start moving toward the vision you've created. Write these down alongside your vision board.

5. **Display Your Board:** Place your vision board somewhere visible as a daily reminder of your goals and aspirations. *Commit to revisiting and updating it regularly as your journey evolves.*

26. Visualizing Your Phoenix Moment

Prompt: What would rising from the ashes look like for you? What habits, mindsets, or people will you leave behind?

Exercise: Close your eyes and visualize your "phoenix moment"—a time when you fully embrace transformation.

Refer to **Feeling Stuck in Life** *to learn about* **The Phoenix Method**

Journal the scene in detail, including what changes you notice in yourself and your environment.

27. (Part 1) Mapping Your Emotional Landscape

This exercise will help you explore your emotions in depth, revealing hidden patterns: guiding you to understand how they shape your daily life.

Step 1: Emotional Report: How do you feel today? Are your emotions clear, cloudy, stormy, or somewhere in between?

Step 2: Charting Peaks and Valleys: Every emotional landscape has peaks (highs) and valleys (lows).
- Write about a time when you felt joy, excitement, or fulfillment.
- Write about a valley, a moment when you felt down, overwhelmed, or stagnant.

<u>Example:</u> One of my emotional peaks happened when... It felt like... A recent emotional valley I experienced was... It felt like...

Step 3: Discover the Hidden Terrain: Sometimes our emotions are rooted in places that we haven't fully explored. Dig deeper and uncover what lies beneath your peaks and valleys.
- Why do certain experiences trigger high or low emotions?
- What patterns are emerging?

Step 4: Emotional Compass: Finding Direction: Calibrate your emotional compass. This compass will help guide you through challenging emotional landscapes in the future.
- What direction do you need to head in when you're navigating difficult emotions?
- What you discovered about your emotional landscape?
- How will you use this awareness to help you navigate stagnation and grow emotionally?

7. Gratitude and Mindfulness

Purpose: This theme focuses on cultivating gratitude and mindfulness, promoting awareness of the present moment and appreciation for personal growth.

Benefits: 1. Mindfulness and gratitude practices will help you to develop a positive perspective. 2. Enhancing resilience and emotional well-being during challenging times.

28. The Gratitude and Growth Jar
29. Mindfulness Check-In

28. The Gratitude and Growth Jar

Prompt: This activity emphasizes the importance of gratitude and self-reflection in overcoming stagnation.

- How can you shift your focus from stagnation to growth?
- What aspects of your life can you celebrate, even in small ways?

Exercise:

1. **Daily Gratitude Practice:** Each day, write down one thing you're grateful for, a small achievement, or a positive experience that reflects your growth. Use colorful paper or post-it notes for a fun touch. *Store these notes in a jar.*

2. **Reflect on Growth:** At the end of each week or month, take time to read through the notes in your jar. *Reflect on how these moments have contributed to your healing journey and progress.*

3. Reflection Questions:

- How does focusing on gratitude shift your mindset regarding stagnation?
- What patterns do you notice in your daily achievements?

4. **Action Step:** As you continue to add to your jar, challenge yourself to seek out new experiences or accomplishments each week. Set a goal for how many notes you want to add by the end of the month.

29. The Mindfulness Check-In

Prompt: How often do you pause to check in with your emotions and physical sensations? What do you notice about your mental and emotional state?

Exercise:

1. **Daily Check-In:** Set aside 5-10 minutes daily to engage in a mindfulness practice. Sit comfortably, close your eyes, and take a few deep breaths. Focus on your body and emotions.

2. **Journaling Reflection:** After the mindfulness practice, write down your observations. **Consider the following:**

   - What emotions did you notice? (Were they positive, negative, or neutral?)
   - How did your body feel?
   - Any areas of tension or relaxation?
   - What patterns do you notice in your emotional state throughout the week?
   - How does checking in with yourself impact your decision-making and reactions to stressors?

8. Overcoming Mental Barriers

Purpose: This theme addresses the mental barriers that can hinder progress, focusing on strategies to acknowledge, confront, and overcome them.

Benefits: Through exercises that promote acknowledgment and accountability, you will learn to break free from cycles of overthinking and self-sabotage, paving the way for personal growth.

30. Breaking Free from the Cycle of Overthinking: Acknowledgment and Accountability

30. Breaking Free from the Cycle of Overthinking: Acknowledgment and Accountability

Prompt: In what areas of your life do you find yourself stuck in overthinking? How does this cycle prevent you from taking action and moving forward?

Exercise:

1. **Acknowledge the Overthinking Cycle:** Reflect on a situation or decision where you've felt paralyzed by overthinking. Write down the situation, the thoughts that keep repeating in your mind, and how this cycle has affected your ability to act.

2. **Identify the Consequences:** Write down the ways in which overthinking has held you back. How has it contributed to stagnation, missed opportunities, or heightened anxiety? *Be specific in identifying the impact it had on your personal and professional life.*

3. **Reflection Questions:**
    - What is one small decision or action you've delayed due to overthinking?
    - What would happen if you took the first step toward resolving the situation, even if it feels uncomfortable or uncertain?

4. **Accountability Plan:** Choose a trusted friend, mentor, or even yourself, to help hold you accountable for breaking free from overthinking.
    - Write down one action that you will take in the next 24 hours to move forward, no matter how small.
    - Share this plan with your accountability partner or journal it to keep track of your progress.

5. **Action Step:** For the next week, whenever you catch yourself overthinking, pause and ask yourself: "What is one action I can take right now to move forward?" Track your responses and actions in your journal, and reflect on how it feels to break free from the cycle of overthinking.

9. Personal Growth and Empowerment

Purpose: This theme will:

- Encourage you to take charge of your personal growth and development.
- Empower you to recognize your strengths and aspirations.

Benefits: By engaging in exercises that promote self-reflection and goal-setting, you will cultivate a sense of agency in your healing journey, and develop a clearer vision for your future.

31. Reframe Your Narrative: Crafting a Life that Reflects Your Strength and Aspirations
32. Realigning Your Positive Replacements

31. Reframe Your Narrative: Crafting a Life That Reflects Your Strength and Aspirations

Prompt: How do you currently view your life story? Does it reflect your strength, resilience, and aspirations, or does it feel tied to past hardships and limitations?

Exercise:

1. **Identify Your Current Narrative:** Write a brief description of your current life story, focusing on **how you see yourself**, and the events that have shaped you. *Be honest about any negative patterns or limiting beliefs that emerge.*

2. **Reframe the Narrative:** Now, rewrite your story from the perspective of your strength and resilience. Highlight moments where you overcame challenges, lessons you've learned, and how these have made you stronger.

3. **Reflection Questions:**
   - What changes did you make when rewriting your story?
   - How does this new narrative make you feel?
   - Does it reflect your goals and the person you want to be?

4. **Action Step:** Write down three actions you can take to align your life with the new narrative you've crafted.

32. Realigning Your Positive Replacements

This exercise will help you to uncover why your positive strategies may not be working, and guide you to realign them.

Step 1: Identify the Negative Quality: Write about the specific negative quality you're trying to overcome. *Be detailed:* Describe how it manifests, when it shows up, and how it makes you feel.

Step 2: Assess Your Positive Replacement: Write about the positive replacement you've been using to address the negative quality. *Reflect on why you chose it.*

- How it has been working?
- Where it may fall short?

Example: The positive replacement I've been using is... I chose this replacement because... It has helped me by... However, it falls short because...

Step 3: Explore the Misalignment: Look deeper into why the positive replacement might not be effective.

- Is it because it doesn't fully address the root cause of the negative quality?
- Is it that you need a more tailored approach?

Write about any misalignments you notice.

Step 4: Reflection: Take a moment to reflect on how realigning your positive strategy can support your healing journey. Write down any insights or feelings that come up during this process.

To understand these activities in its entirety, please refer to the corresponding book:

Feeling Stuck in Life: Breaking Free Brick by Brick